Roven Grace Simpson Thomas

Number   5587293

First published in the UK by
HarperCollins Children's Books in 2010
1 3 5 7 9 10 8 6 4 2
ISBN: 978-0-00-736510-4

A CIP catalogue record for this title is available
from the British Library.
No part of this publication may be reproduced, stored in a
retrieval system or transmitted in any form or by any means,
electronic, mechanical, photocopying, recording or otherwise
without the prior permission of HarperCollins Publishers Ltd,
77-85 Fulham Palace Road, Hammersmith, London, W6 8JB.

The HarperCollins website address is:
www.harpercollins.co.uk

Printed and bound in China

Hello Kitty

Guide to Parties

HarperCollins *Children's Books*

I love parties – what girl doesn't? They're a fabulous way to celebrate all sorts of occasions with your friends and family, at any time of year! Nothing beats the feeling of excitement you get before a big bash you've been looking forward to for ages.

Planning your own party is super exciting. Anybody can do it – you just need to be organised. I've crammed as many tips as possible into my Guide to Parties, from making themed decorations, planning fun games and choosing your food and drinks menu, to creating the perfect party atmosphere with music and lighting. Oh, and most importantly, putting together a killer outfit!

I've also included my post-party tips for cleaning up, writing thank you notes and recording your party memories, as well as creative card and present ideas for friends' parties and hints on how to be the perfect guest.

So, whether you're a VIP guest or hosting your own bash, this guide will help you make the most of every party. Enjoy!

Lots of love,

Hello Kitty
X

Contents

Throwing a party:

the basics

Type of party

So, you want to throw a party? What a fabulous idea! If you want it to be a success, you need to get planning asap. Follow my simple step-by-step guide to help you make those all-important initial decisions.

First things first – you need to choose what type of party you would like to throw. (We'll get to your outfit later!)

Will you be celebrating your birthday with friends? Are you planning a surprise party for someone special? Or will it be a super-scary Halloween party? Any excuse will do!

To get you started, here's a list of my favourite occasions to throw a party:

* **Birthday**
* **End of Term**
* **Valentine's Day**
* **Easter**
* **Summer**
* **Halloween**
* **Christmas Eve**
* **New Year's Eve**
* **House-warming**
* **Just because you feel like it!**

Where and when?

Now you have the occasion sorted, the next step is to pick your venue. You may want to hire a venue for your bash, but this can be pricey.

I love throwing parties at my house! It's much cheaper, and I can really go all-out with the decorations and personalise everything to my taste. If you decide to stay at home you can invite friends to sleep over afterwards so they don't have to worry about getting home. Consider how much space you have and how many people you'd like to invite before committing to a house party though, and make sure you check with everyone else who lives with you.

Also, bear in mind that if the weather's warm enough, you can take the party out into your garden to give you more space and a summery atmosphere.

Now, pick a date and time. Make sure it's convenient for everybody – I usually have my parties on Saturday afternoons/evenings when I know everyone can make it, but the start time will depend on the type of party you're having: tea parties work best in the afternoon, Halloween parties will be spookier after dark, and sleepovers might go on all night (if you can stay awake, that is!)

What type of party should you throw?

Parties are a great excuse to hang out with your favourite people, eat yummy food and dance the night away to your favourite tunes! But sometimes deciding exactly what kind of party to throw can be tricky. Take this quiz to reveal your perfect choice of party:

1. You're organising your birthday bash. What do you think about first?

A – Your outfit – you will be the centre of attention and need to look fantastic!

B – The music – after all, what is a party without music?

C – The food – it's essential for you to have lots of tasty treats for your guests to enjoy.

D – The entertainment – you want to make sure everyone has a great time!

2. You're really excited about your party, but who do you invite?

A – Your entire class at school – you can all get excited together that way.

B – Everyone you know – this will be the social event of the year!

C – Your very best friends – girls only!

D – Your close friends and family – you want to see the people that matter most on this special occasion.

3. You're shopping for party food. What's on the menu?

A – Themed food, such as slime jelly and spaghetti worms for a super-scary bash!

B – Mini finger food – so you can eat and dance on the go.

C – Sweets, chocolate, popcorn and pizza – perfect for a midnight feast.

D – Jelly and ice cream – you're never too old for this delicious combo!

4. Now for the biggest dilemma of all! What will you wear to make sure all eyes are on you?

 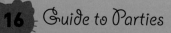

A – Your handmade fairy costume – it's sure to turn a few heads!

B – You're going all-out this time – glittery party dress, high heels and lots of sparkly jewellery.

C – Your comfiest pyjamas and fluffiest slippers – perfect for a girlie night in.

D – The lovely new skirt and top you got for your birthday.

5. It's almost party time. What special surprise have you planned to make your party go with a bang?

A – You've decked the whole venue out to look like a haunted house, complete with cobwebs and a full-size skeleton!

B – You've hired a top DJ to play fabulous music all night long.

C – You've made special cards so everyone can play 'Truth or Dare?'

D – Popular party games – pass the parcel and musical chairs are always great fun!

Mostly As – You should throw a Fancy Dress Festivity!

There's nothing you love more than dressing up in cool costumes and going to a fun themed night. Whether it's princesses, pirates, heroes and villains or Wild West, this is definitely the kind of party you and your friends will love.

Mostly Bs – You should throw a Disco Do!

What could be better than looking super-stylish and dancing the night away to your favourite music under the disco lights? You've been waiting for a chance to show off those new moves, and now it's here. Release your inner disco-diva!

Mostly Cs – You should throw a Super Sleepover!

Gather up your sleeping bags and make yourself comfortable, it's time for a girlie night in! Fill this fun night with makeovers, movies and tasty treats and it's sure to be a great success. Why not challenge yourselves to see who can stay awake longest?

Mostly Ds – You should throw a Traditional Tea Party!

These afternoon gatherings are a fantastic way to entertain both family and friends, and are always heaps of fun. My favourite part is giving my friends a goody bag to take home, stuffed full of delicious birthday cake and other fab surprises!

Themes

Themed parties are super fun! I always choose a theme for my parties, no matter what the occasion. There are so many to choose from I never run out of ideas. Here are some of my favourite themes to give you a little inspiration.

Love is in the Air – ideal for Valentine's Day.

Afternoon Tea – good old English tea parties will never go out of style.

Pirates – swashbuckling fun for any time of year.

Karaoke – great fun, whether you can sing or not!

Disco Ball – dance the night away with your friends to some hot disco tunes!

Fashion Swap – perfect for picking up some new outfits and getting rid of some old ones!

Wild West – every girl looks good in cowboy boots and a denim skirt!

Hollywood – I always dress up as Marilyn.

Tube Stations – I live in London so this is one of my absolute favourites! Dressing as a tube station is great fun!

Winter Wonderland – guaranteed to add some sparkle to the colder months.

Rainbow Colours – perfect for snapping some fantastic photos!

Hawaii – limbo competition, anyone?

Sleepover – a great opportunity for a girlie gossip and a midnight feast.

80s – another blast-from-the-past theme you can really have fun with.

Movie Premiere – ask your friends to dress up for the premiere, pick a DVD everybody wants to see and host your very own screening!

Once you've decided on a theme, you can choose food, decorations and, of course, an outfit that fits with it. Mention the theme clearly in your invitations, and ask your guests to dress up too. You could even hold a costume competition to encourage everybody to make that extra effort, and pick a cool themed prize for the winner!

Party Countdown

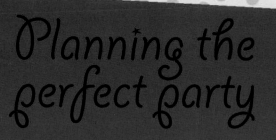

Planning the perfect party

So you've decided what kind of party you're going to throw, where and when it will be, and you've picked your theme. Now you need to get down to planning the most fabulous bash ever! After all, you and your guests deserve a fantastic night, and there are lots of things to think about.

Planning is so much fun! It's also essential to any successful party, so it's a good job I love making lists! What will really make your party special is attention to detail. Your guests will notice, and appreciate it. So you need to give yourself at least three weeks to plan properly.

Do you have lots of ideas for your party but don't know where to begin? Or perhaps you're lacking inspiration and need some tips to get the ball rolling? Whatever stage you're at, find yourself a stylish note-book, grab a pen, and let's get started!

Three weeks to go!

The guest list

• Think about the space you will be using for your party and how many people you can realistically fit into it.

• Only invite people you want to see. If there's someone you'd rather not invite, don't feel pressured into it. Space will probably be limited, and it's your party!

• Don't worry if your guests come from different friendship groups and don't know each other, you can introduce them on the night and watch as new friendships form!

• For a house party, remember to invite your neighbours, if you know them.

Guest list

for Hello Kitty's Christmas Eve bash:

♡ Mimmy

♡ Mama

♡ Papa

♡ Dear Daniel

♡ Fifi

♡ Rory

♡ Joey

♡ Thomas

♡ Jodie

♡ Tracy

♡ Tim and Tammy

♡ Tippy

♡ Ben

♡ Alice

♡ Milton

♡ Karen

♡ ~~Charlotte~~

♡ William

♡ Phil

♡ Chris

♡ Helen

♡ Edward

♡ Anthony

♡ Simon

Invitations

You can send your party invitations online or by post, or give them out by hand. I love being creative, so I always design my own invitations for my parties. I create them on my computer, print them off, cut them into a shape and decorate them, then post them out to my guests. Why don't you give it a go?

Make your invitations as interesting and eye-catching as possible. Check out some of mine to give you some ideas:

Pirate party
at Hello Kitty's House

Date: 7th June from six PM til midnight.

Dress code: Walk the plank!

RSVP: 0567 333 131 by 24th May.

Spooky Halloween Bash
at Hello Kitty's Haunted Mansion

Date: 31st October from six PM til midnight

Dress code: Come dressed as your favourite dead celebrity!

RSVP: 0567 333 131 by 17th October.

Valentine's Day Party
at Hello Kitty's House of Love

Date: 14th February,
from seven PM til midnight.

Dress code: Pretty in pink,
radiant in red!

RSVP: 0567 333 131
by 31st January

Hello Kitty's Christmas Eve Party
at Hello Kitty's House

Date: 24th December,
from 4PM til 11PM.

Dress code: Festive!

RSVP: 0567 333 131
by 10th December

Hello Kitty

Hello Kitty's Fabulous Birthday Bash

at Hello Kitty's House

Date: 1st November, from six PM til midnight

Dress code: Hollywood icons!

RSVP: 0567 333 131 by 18th October

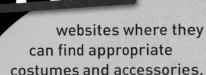

Make sure you include the following information on your invitation:
• Your name (as the host)
• Type of party, e.g. birthday party, surprise party etc
• Venue (e.g. your home address in full, with directions and map on a separate sheet if necessary)
• Date and start/finish times
• Dress code: be specific so that nobody is confused. If you ask your guests to dress up, suggest shops or websites where they can find appropriate costumes and accessories.
• Your email, phone, and/or address for the RSVP. Choose an RSVP deadline that gives you at least two weeks to plan everything.
• Any other relevant information, e.g. will there be a costume competition? Should your guests bring sleeping bags with them if you are having a sleepover?

Guide to Parties

Two weeks to go!

Budget and equipment

By now your guest list should be finalised. How exciting! If anybody hasn't RSVPd yet, give them a quick call or instant message them so you can get a final number and start planning properly.

Set your budget before you begin shopping for supplies, but after you have finalised your guest list. That way you'll know how much you have to spend per head and won't accidentally blow everything on the decorations, as tempting as it might be! Remember to agree the amount in advance with anybody else who might be involved.

Bearing in mind your final head count, think about which rooms you will be using for the party, and which you would like to keep off limits (you need some privacy, after all!)

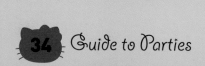

Next you need to make a note of how many chairs, tables and usable surfaces you have, and where they might best be set up. You will need plenty of seats, a surface on which to serve your delicious food and drinks, and possibly a gift table, if you're expecting lots of presents!

Will you need to borrow anything from a neighbour or friend?

Some people will want to sit and chat, whilst others will be happy to dance the night away! Make sure you leave plenty of floor space whilst also providing comfy chairs/sofas for people who need a dancing break.

Check out how much fridge, freezer and oven space you have. If you want to prepare a lot of the food yourself and space is limited, a nearby friend or neighbour may let you use their kitchen on the day as well.

You'll need a sound system in the main room, and a suitable spot to sit it in (away from food and drink to avoid risk of damage). If you don't own one, ask a friend or relative if you can borrow theirs.

How many plates, bowls, serving platters etc do you have? You can either use what you have and risk breakages, or buy disposable options instead. Again, remember to ask permission if the crockery doesn't belong to you. If you decide to buy disposable options, party stores sell lots of themed sets (plates, bowls, glasses etc) which are always a fun option!

Party style and beauty ideas

Here comes the best bit! I'm sure you're really keen to start planning your outfit and general party look, so get hold of as many hair, beauty and fashion magazines as you can, curl up on the sofa for the afternoon and read through them, cutting out any articles that interest you. I keep a scrapbook full of hair and beauty tips, fabulous outfits and style advice to inspire me.

Once you have a general idea of the look you want to go for, check through your wardrobe to see what workable outfits you already have and what you might need to buy. I have a costume box next to my wardrobe that's full of bits and pieces: hats, costume jewellery and clothes and accessories from previous parties. I often dip into this when putting together a new party outfit.

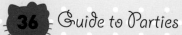

Check through all your beauty and make-up products and make a list of all the supplies you will need to get thoroughly glammed up! Think about the beauty treatments you want to give yourself in the run up to the big day, the make-up you'd like to wear and the hairstyle you want to create.

Food and drink

Time to plan your food and drinks menu – yummy! I like to serve buffet food at my parties. It's easy to eat standing up as well as sitting down, and you can provide a much wider variety of options than if you plan a sit-down dinner.

Remember to serve food that fits with your theme. So, for example, if you are throwing a Halloween party, you could serve food that looks like eyeballs, worms and severed fingers. Disgusting!

Obviously you will need to buy some items, such as crisps, but you might want to make a few dishes yourself. Go through your recipe books and mark or photocopy the pages you will need, or do some recipe research online. Make a note of all the ingredients you will need to buy, as well as any ready-made foods you will be buying. Check out the food and drink shopping list from my last birthday party:

- Four large bags salted nachos
- Four large bags crisps, assorted flavours
- Two tubs of hummus
- Two tubs of guacamole
- Two tubs of sour cream and chive dip
- Two bags carrot batons
- Two large bags celery
- Two French sticks
- One pack butter
- Large cheddar cheese
- Pineapple cubes
- Cocktail sticks

- Two bags red grapes
- Two packs sausage rolls
- Two packs scotch eggs
- Two large quiches, one vegetarian
- Two packs mini pizzas, assorted
- Two packs party rings
- One large tin chocolates
- Ingredients for cake
- Candles for cake
- Ingredients for mocktails

Mocktail and fruit punch recipes

Mocktails and non-alcoholic punches are yummy, and healthy too. Plus they make perfect party drinks as they are so colourful! Here are some of my favourite recipes:

Mocktails

You will need a cocktail shaker and highball glasses to make these.

Sour Mix

1 cup caster sugar
2 cups water
2 cups freshly squeezed lemon juice

Stir together well. Keeps in the fridge for up to 7 days.

The Cuban Cooler

10 fresh mint leaves
20ml liquid sugar or honey
20ml fresh lemon juice
40ml cloudy apple juice
20ml cranberry juice

Freeze water in a plastic container overnight (or get ready-made ice cubes), wrap the block of ice in a kitchen towel and smash the block with a rolling-pin to make crushed ice. Squeeze the lemon juice freshly. Add the mint leaves and the sugar or honey to a highball glass and muddle the leaves (bruise them gently to release the oil in the leaves). Add the crushed ice, apple and lemon juice to the glass and stir. Top up with cranberry juice and garnish with a lemon or lime wedge.

Virgin Margarita
1 part orange juice
1 part lime juice
3 parts sour mix

(A part can be any quantity you like as long as it is the same quantity for all the ingredients.)
Fill a cocktail shaker with ice. Add the ingredients and shake well. Strain into an ice-filled highball glass and top up with lemonade.

Shirley Temple
Ginger ale
Grenadine
A wedge of lemon

Fill a highball glass with ice. Add a couple of dashes of grenadine, then fill to the top with ginger ale. Squeeze the juice from the lemon wedge into the drink, and garnish with a cherry.

Cranpina
70ml cranberry juice
70ml pink grapefruit juice
70ml pineapple juice
30ml fresh orange juice

Fill a highball glass with ice cubes. Pour the first three ingredients into the glass and stir. Then add the orange juice - it will sink slowly down the glass as you drink it, but will look fabulous when you first serve it!

Passnshoot
Mango
Passhion
Pineapple
orange
Juce

Fruit Punch
4 cups Ginger Ale
2 cups fruit syrup
2 cups pineapple juice
2 cups sugar
3 cups water
1 cup hot decaf green tea (or herbal tea)
1 cup lemon juice
1 cup cherries

Method:
Boil the water and mix in the sugar until it has completely dissolved. Next, add the syrup, pineapple juice and lemon juice and mix thoroughly. Then add the tea. Put it in the fridge until it has cooled down. Once it has cooled, add the cherries and the ginger ale and serve in a pretty punch bowl. Remember to add ice to keep the punch cool.
You might want to decorate your punch bowl with slices of fruit, too.

Cakes

A party wouldn't be a party without a cake! I love baking, and cakes are one of my specialities. Here are two of my favourite recipes – you might like to try them out:
(Younger Hello Kitty fans should always ask an adult to help them.)

Chocolate no cook cake

Lightly oil a tin that measures 18x18cm, then line it with cling film, leaving enough hanging over the rim to wrap up the cake entirely.

Melt 350g plain chocolate, broken into pieces, with 150g unsalted butter in a large bowl resting over a pan of just-boiled water. Make sure the bowl doesn't touch the water.

When both have melted, add 175g digestive biscuits, broken into smallish pieces and up to 300g mixed dried fruit, marshmallows or nuts.

Mix everything together. Spoon the cake mixture into the prepared tin, tapping it once or twice to allow the mixture to settle, then level the surface.

Seal up in the cling film and chill for at least 6 hours (overnight is better).

To serve, turn the cake onto a board and peel off the cling film.

Cut into thick slices.

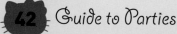

Vanilla Cupcakes

Ingredients
125g caster sugar
125g unsalted butter, very soft
2 eggs
2 tsp vanilla essence
150g plain flour
2 tsp baking powder

How to make
1. Preheat the oven to 180C/Gas mark 4.
2. Beat the sugar and butter until light and fluffy.
3. Add the beaten eggs and vanilla (don't worry if it looks curdled, the flour will fix this).
4. Sift in the flour and baking powder and mix thoroughly.
5. Spoon into eight muffin cups placed in the pockets of a muffin tray.
6. Bake for 20-25 minutes until golden and firm.
7. Leave to cool.

Icing

Ingredients
100g icing sugar
60g full-fat cream cheese
35g butter (room temperature)

How to make
1. Beat the butter and sugar together until the butter is fully mixed in.
2. Add the cream cheese and mix until everything is combined – don't mix too hard as the cheese may split.

Add to the top of the muffins, and finish off with sweets!

The perfect party atmosphere

What kind of atmosphere do you want to create for your party? Classy and relaxed for a tea party? Vibrant and upbeat for an 80s disco? Or totally spooky for a Halloween bash? There are lots of simple ways to achieve the perfect atmosphere. Here are my top tips:

Lighting

I love to use candles, coloured lights or fairy lights to set the mood indoors. If you'll be using your garden as well, patio heaters and lantern lights can look fabulous.

If you want your guests to feel lively and full of energy, use brighter lighting. If you want to encourage dancing, go darker but use flashing disco lights.

You can also set the mood by hanging sheets of coloured fabric over lamps to create a coloured glow. I like to use pink on Valentine's Day and red on Halloween!

Decorations

There are so many to choose from! Make a list of everything you'll need for your chosen theme. Here are my must-haves for all the classic party occasions:

Christmas: tinsel, mistletoe, holly, and a Christmas tree, of course!

Halloween: cobwebs, skeleton, pumpkins, bats, spiders

Valentine's Day: red roses, heart-shaped confetti, red and pink fabric, lots of candles

Birthday: balloons, streamers, Happy Birthday banner

Easter: yellow chicks, white bunnies, coloured paper (to make bunny footprints), coloured eggs, egg hunt kit, daffodils

And here are some decorations lists I made recently for some of my themed parties:

Decorations for Pirate Party

- Two large skeletons dressed in pirates' clothes
- Brown paper (to make wall look like side of ship)
- 30 eye patches to hand out to guests
- 30 swords
- 30 bandanas
- Plastic treasure chests x 6, in which to put:
  Chocolate coins
  Plastic beads x 20
  Fake rings/jewels x 20

Decorations for Hawaiian Party

- Hawaiian table skirt x 2
- Hawaiian table confetti
- Hanging parrots x 6
- Palm tree garland
- Inflatable palm trees x 4
- Bamboo limbo set

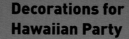
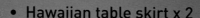

See? It's really easy to set the scene, and decorations come at very affordable prices – you just have to be prepared to shop around.

Music

Every party needs a soundtrack packed with party hits. The music you play will really affect the mood of your party, so choose carefully.

If you want people to dance, make a playlist of pop and dance tracks and crank up the volume. Not too loud though, you don't want the neighbours to complain! Remember to include classics as well as newer tracks so there's something for everyone.

If you're throwing a Christmas party, you'll have no problem finding hundreds of festive tunes to get you all in the mood for the holidays.

If you want people to mingle and chat, create a compilation of relaxing background music and set the volume slightly lower.

Hosting a Valentine's Day party? Love is in the air so search your collection for big ballads and romantic love songs. Aah.

If your party has a theme, try to find music that fits. For example, if you're throwing an English tea party, go for classical music. If you're throwing a Wild West party, stick on some country and western. If you don't own any suitable music yourself, your parents might be able to help you!

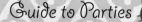

Games

A party wouldn't be a party without games! Here are some of my favourites:

Truth or Dare?

Sit in a circle and pick someone to start. Ask them the question, 'Truth or Dare?' If they pick 'truth', they must pick a 'truth' card and answer the question printed on it. If they pick 'dare' they must choose a 'dare' card and carry out the dare printed on it. Everyone takes it in turns to have a go. If players refuse to complete their truth or dare, they are out. The winner is the last person left in.

Ideal for:
any occasion!

You will need:
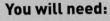 pre-prepared cards with questions and dares printed on them (I usually print these from my computer)
Try to think of funny truth questions and dares that your friends won't be too embarrassed to do.

Matching Characters

Pick famous couples, such as Brad and Angelina, Romeo and Juliet, Bella and Edward, etc. Write each individual name on a sticky note. Ask everyone to pick a note without looking and stick it to their forehead.
The object of the game is to guess who you are as quickly as possible by asking simple 'yes/no' questions, such as, 'Am I alive?' 'Am I female?' 'Am I English?' The winners are the first couple to both guess who they are and find each other!

Ideal for:
any occasion, but particularly suitable for Valentine's Day!

Spin the Bottle of Nail Varnish

Arrange the bottles of nail varnish in a circle and place the empty plastic bottle in the centre.
Take it in turns to spin the bottle until it stops, and take the bottle of varnish it is pointing towards.
Paint one of your nails using the varnish.
Continue taking it in turns to spin the bottle until everyone has painted all their fingernails (you can also play using your toenails, of course). You'll get some interesting colour combinations!

You will need:
★ nail varnish in various colours
★ an empty plastic bottle

Ideal for:
girlie sleepovers. Girls will love this game, but if the boys are keen as well, it can be doubly entertaining!

You will need:
* ★ four buckets, two large, two medium-size
* ★ two large sponges
* ★ water

Sponge Relay

Set up the two medium-size buckets at the 'starting line' and the two large buckets directly opposite them, at least 30 feet away, depending on how much space you have. Fill the two farthest buckets to the brim with water. Divide your guests into two teams.

The first player from each team takes a sponge and runs to the farthest buckets, dips the sponge in the water, runs back to the starting line and squeezes the water into the empty bucket, then passes the sponge to the next person.

The first team to completely fill their bucket with water wins!

Ideal for: summer garden parties!

Blind Make-over

Ideal for:
girlie
sleepovers

Pick a person to blindfold.
This person will be the
make-up artist!
Pick another person to be
the model.
The person in the blindfold
must apply make-up to the model and see
how well they do!
Take it in turns until everybody has had a go.
Remember to take lots of photos during
this one!

You will need:
★ make-up
★ a blindfold

Apple Bobbing

Set up two bowls filled with water and
put apples into each bowl.
Divide your guests into two teams.
Without using their hands, each
team member must bob for an
apple and catch it in their mouth,
then remove it from the bowl.
The winning team is the first team
to catch all their apples.
This one can get messy so girls
wearing make-up might not be so
keen to take part...

Ideal for:
Halloween

You will need:
★ two bowls
★ water
★ apples

Mummy Wrap

Ideal for:
Halloween

You will need:
★ toilet rolls

Divide your guests into two teams.
Choose one person from each team
to be the 'Mummy'.
On the count of three, the teams start
to wrap their respective 'Mummy' in
toilet roll.
The first team to completely cover
their Mummy in toilet roll wins.
Again, remember your camera for
this one!

Dance-off

Ideal for:
every party!

You will need:
★ space for
dancing and
a killer playlist.

Host a dance-off to see
who has the best moves.
Your guests can take it in turns
to dance-off with each other.
Winner stays on each time until
everybody has taken a turn. The
rest of the guests decide who
wins each round.
You can make a certificate and rosette to
present to the winner, and give them a
prize of your choosing too!

Costume competition

If you have asked your guests to wear costumes, judge the costumes throughout the night and at the end of the party, announce the winners! You can make certificates and rosettes for third, second and first place and buy a theme-related prize for the overall winner.

If you're stuck for ideas when creating your certificates, try following my example here:

This certificate is awarded to

....

For winner of Best Costume at

Hello Kitty's Hawaiian party

Date 27th June

Congratulations!

Tip: mention the costume competition on your invitation and I guarantee your guests will make the extra effort!

Your outfit

Planning and putting together your party outfit is, without a doubt, the best bit of your party preparations! Every girl loves to dress up and look fabulous, and you want all eyes to be on you on your special night. Here are some outfits I've put together that won't fail to wow:

Cowgirl

Pick out a blue denim skirt. Find some cowboy boots (brown or tan work well). Get yourself a checked western-style shirt if you really want to look authentic. Or you could wear a simple white vest or T-shirt with a denim waistcoat. You can buy cowboy hats and other accessories such as pistols from most party and accessory shops.

You can also make your own Sheriff badge. All you need is silver cardboard, sticky tape, a safety pin, a marker pen and scissors. Draw a star shape on the card, write the word 'Sheriff' in the middle, cut it out, stick the safety pin securely onto the back and pin onto your top.

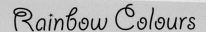

Rainbow Colours

This theme is great fun. You can pick any colour of the rainbow and dress yourself in it from head to toe, or you can go in every colour of the rainbow! I like to pick one colour, and ask six friends to do the same, so together we make a rainbow. Last time I was indigo!

A dress, a skirt and top, jeans and a vest...you can wear whatever you like, as long as it's the right colour!

Remember to pick accessories in the same colour. To really complete your look, opt for coloured eye shadow and, if possible, lip gloss!

Movie Premiere

One of my favourite themes! You can get all glammed up in your favourite dress and heels for this one. You can even accessorise with a fabulous hat, funky fascinator or a pretty pashmina. Sparkly jewellery works well for this theme, too. You might want to dress up as your favourite actor instead.

Hawaii

If you're feeling a little shy, you can always wear a colourful summer vest over your bikini top. You can buy flower garlands from costume and accessory shops. I like to wear them round my neck, wrists and ankles, and fasten one large flower to the side of my head!

You will need
- a bikini
- a grass skirt
- lots of flowers!

Devilish Devil

It goes without saying that for this costume you should wear red! A little red dress is the perfect devilish outfit.

You can either buy yourself an accessories kit, containing horns, a tail and a pitchfork, or make your own.

You will need

- A black cotton hairband (as thin as possible)
- Red felt material
- Needle and red thread
- Red ribbon
- A stick, branch or old brush handle (approximately two feet long)
- Three smaller sticks or dowels (approximately four inches long)
- Glue and sticky tape

- Cut out two horn-shapes from the red felt.
- Sew them onto your cotton hairband.
- For the tail, cut a piece of red felt about 2 feet long and 2-3 inches wide.
- Lie the material on a flat surface. Put a line of cotton balls down the middle of the tail from top to bottom, then sew up.
- Now cut a triangular piece of red felt about half the size of your palm and sew it to the end of the tail.
- For the pitchfork, wrap the longer stick in red ribbon so that it is completely covered, sticking the ends down with glue or sticky tape.
- Do the same with the smaller sticks or dowels.
- Then stick one smaller stick/dowel across the top of the large stick. At each end of this, stick the other small sticks to make a fork shape.

Snow Queen

You will need
• a dress in either white or silver (you can either use something you already have and accessorise it up or buy a dress from a costume shop).

For the accessories
• a crown/tiara and a wand. Costume shops will sell lots of affordable options.

This is a really fun costume to put together. Use cold, icy colours for your make-up such as blues, silvers, whites and pinks.
A glittery eye shadow and lip gloss will really finish off your look.
Girls with pale skin will really suit this costume.

Christmas Elf

With the right accessories, you can wear anything red or green for this outfit, but costume shops stock some fantastic little elf dresses!
For your make-up, concentrate on giving yourself rosy red cheeks and lips.
Try blending some red lipstick onto your cheeks for maximum effect.

Must-have accessories
- an elf hat
- green or red tights
- thick black belt with a large square buckle

(all of which you can pick up at costume shops.)

What's your party style?

Still not sure what to wear? Take this quiz and find your perfect party style!

1. You're getting ready for a friend's birthday party. What do you think about first?

A – Your hair and make-up – you want to look as elegant as possible for the fancy do.

B – Calling your friends to check what they are wearing – you don't want to be underdressed!

C – Planning your outfit – the most important thing!

2. You've decided to wear your best outfit to the party. What is it?

A – A classy dress and heels, with lots of co-ordinating jewellery.

B – Your favourite jeans and a trendy top – you can always rely on them to look great!

C – The 1950s movie star outfit you made especially for this Hollywood themed bash.

3. What gift have you bought the host for their birthday?

A – You've gone all out and bought her an adorable necklace and matching earring set.

B – You've customised a T-shirt you know she will love.

C – You've been creative and baked her a batch of personalised cupcakes instead!

4. What's your idea of a fashion nightmare at a party?

A – Spilling a drink all over your sassy new dress.

B – Putting on those wobbly high heels you can't really walk in.

C – Turning up in the same outfit as someone else – you wanted to be original!

5. How would you describe your everyday style?

A – You dress to impress and always make an effort – you never know who you might meet!

B – You love to wear denim – simple and stylish.

C – Creative and unique, you love one-off items that make you stand out from the crowd.

Mostly As – You're a glamour girl!
If there's a party going on, you know it's time to get that posh dress out of your wardrobe and step out in style! You love to make the most of looking fabulous Whether it's accessorising with snazzy jewellery or making sure your hair is perfectly styled, you always end up looking party-perfect.

Mostly Bs – You're casual cool!
There's nothing wrong with a laid-back look, but parties are special occasions and a time for looking your best. Why not jazz up your usual jeans and top with a funky scarf or a colourful cardi? Remember to add some cute pumps for a casual chic look!

Mostly Cs – You're a fancy-dress fashionista!
To you, parties are a chance to show off your unique style. Costume parties are your favourites, as you really have a chance to get creative and wear something that no-one else will. Why? Because you designed it yourself, of course!

Shopping list

Time to shop for the bulk of your party items!

Your shopping list might look something like this:

- Your outfit, accessories, make-up etc

- Ready-made decorations (remember to bring the decorations list you made earlier)

- Materials you will need to create your own decorations

- Sticky tape, adhesive putty, string etc

- Prizes for competitions (e.g. costume competition, dance-off)

- Plates, glasses, cutlery (real or disposable), straws, table covers if needed

- Ice cube trays or bags. You might want to buy shaped ice cube trays that complement your theme. They are very cheap and come in all sorts of shapes: hearts, skull and crossbones, letters of the alphabet, lips, guitars – anything you like! Shop online for a fantastic range of options.

- Non-perishable food and drink items (see your food and drink shopping list, but don't buy anything with a short expiry date yet as it will most likely go off before the party)

- Non-perishable cake ingredients

- Toilet rolls!

- Bin bags

- Cleaning products such as washing-up liquid, carpet cleaner etc

One week to go!

Creative decorations

Here are some fab ideas that you might want to use:

If it's a surprise party for a frien (and I hope you've managed to keep it a secret no matter how excited you are!) you could print off photos of him or her and ma garlands out of them. This work particularly well if you print off photos at a large size and cut ou just their heads!

Time to get creative! Even if you have bought decorations you can always make more, or customise them to really reflect your personality.

If it's a Wild West party, make yourself some 'Wanted' posters using pictures of your friends and put them up on your walls. You could also make a 'Saloon' sign for your living room or kitchen door.

If it's a Tube Stations party, make signs for different stations to stick around your house. I like to use the funniest-sounding names, such as 'Angel', 'Seven Sisters' and 'Wapping'. You could also make a 'Way out' sign for your door, and signs for different tube lines going into different rooms, such as 'Northern Line', 'Circle Line' and 'Jubilee Line'.

For a Hollywood party, try designing stars for your very own 'star walk' using friends' names. Stick them on your floors and encourage friends to hunt for theirs. If you're feeling really creative, you could design your own 'Hollywood' sign for your wall, based on the real one in LA!

Signs

Now is the perfect time for you to make any signs you might need for the big night, such as the ones I made below:

Hello Kitty's
Fabulous Fashion-Swap Party inside!

Hello Kitty's
BEDROOM
KEEP OUT!

Hello Kitty
Coats & Bags

Music

You should already have thought about the mood you want to create with your music. Here are my top tips on how to create the perfect playlist:

Unless you're hiring a DJ (or your older brother's friends have offered to come round with their decks) you'll need to make a party playlist for your computer or MP3 Player, or collect all the CDs you want to use and put them in your chosen play order.

Unless your party has a very specific musical theme, include a mixture of genres: pop, rock, dance and R 'n B are always popular, and include classics as well as newer tracks. It's best to start off up tempo, move into dance and then slow down for the end of the party.

Before the party, ask your friends to request their favourite party tracks, and add these to your playlist.

Make sure you have enough party tracks to keep people entertained for the whole night. Borrow as many CDs as you can from friends and family to give you a variety of artists.

Preparing your pad

You'll spend a lot of time making yourself look gorgeous for your big bash, but your house or venue will need to look its best too. As well as your designated party rooms, some guests may want a guided tour of the house, and your bathroom will be in constant use throughout your party. So, you need to give the whole house a thorough clean – your family will love you for this!

You will need to do a final clean on the day of the party, but it's a good idea to get the bigger jobs out of the way now, such as cleaning the bathroom, vacuuming and mopping all your floors and giving every room a thorough dust.

Cleaning can be boring, so invite a couple of friends over to help the weekend before the party, stick on your favourite playlist and your pad will look like a palace in no time!

Remember to clear out your coat closet or find somewhere suitable for guests to leave their coats and bags.
You might also want to remove any valuable/breakable items and store them somewhere safe!

Guide to Parties

A few days to go!

Checklist: venue and menu

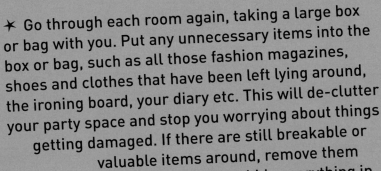

Venue

★ Go through each room in the house and empty all the bins.

★ Go through each room again, taking a large box or bag with you. Put any unnecessary items into the box or bag, such as all those fashion magazines, shoes and clothes that have been left lying around, the ironing board, your diary etc. This will de-clutter your party space and stop you worrying about things getting damaged. If there are still breakable or valuable items around, remove them now. You can then hide everything in a spare bedroom or the loft.

Menu

✦ Time to shop for all the perishable food you will need. Make a detailed list based on your chosen menu.

✦ Fill your freezer with ice cubes – you can never have too much ice at a party!

✦ Prepare as much food and drink as you can now. Then, make a list of things you will need to sort on the day of the party and stick it to your fridge!

Checklist: you!

Hang your outfit on your wardrobe door and your accessories ready on your dressing table.

Check through your beauty and make-up supplies to make sure you have everything you need. Here's a checklist of items you might use whilst getting ready:

Body

- ♡ Body exfoliating scrub
- ♡ Body moisturiser
- ♡ Nail varnish
- ♡ Nail varnish remover
- ♡ Foot scrub
- ♡ Foot file
- ♡ Perfume
- ♡ Shimmery body dust or cream
- ♡ Nail file
- ♡ Nail clippers

Face

- ♡ Face mask (purifying if you have oily skin, moisturising if you have dry skin)
- ♡ Cleanser
- ♡ Toner
- ♡ Moisturiser
- ♡ Tweezers
- ♡ Cotton pads
- ♡ Cotton buds
- ♡ Make-up
- ♡ Make-up remover
- ♡ Eye primer (great if you'll be wearing a dark eye shadow that may crease)

Hair

- ♡ Intensive hair conditioner
- ♡ Hair brush
- ♡ Comb
- ♡ Heat-protective spray
- ♡ Hair dryer
- ♡ Hair straighteners or curling tongs
- ♡ Hair spray or mousse

You'll want to look absolutely stunning for the big day, so invite your friends over, ideally the afternoon or evening before, and pamper yourselves with the beauty treatments you have bought. If everybody brings a few products you'll have plenty of choice. You might decide to give yourselves manicures and pedicures the night before the big party, but if you'll risk chipping your nail varnish it's best to wait and do your manicure on the day.

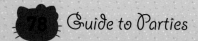 *Guide to Parties*

Party time!

Last-minute preparations

The big day has finally arrived! Excited? You should be!

If they aren't there already, get on the phone and invite one or two friends round to help you with all the last-minute preparations – it'll be much quicker with company. Then you can get ready together too, which is half the fun!

Last-minute checklist

- Put up all your decorations. You might need: sticky tape, adhesive putty or string, depending on what your decorations are

- Hang balloons and a sign outside your house, so anybody who hasn't visited you before knows they are at the right place!

- Put up the rest of your signs, e.g. for the coat closet, bathroom, and a 'Keep out' sign for your bedroom

- Put plenty of hand towels in your bathroom for guests, and double-check that you have enough soap and toilet roll

- Go round each room with a box one more time and put any unnecessary items into it, then store it with the rest of the items you have already hidden

- Set up your party lights, candles etc

- Set up your sound system

- Charge your camera!

Food and drink

Check your list of food still to be prepared. Overestimate any cooking times as something is bound to go wrong, and remember to leave time to clean up any mess you make.

Once all your party food is ready, arrange it on plates, in bowls etc, covered with cling film in your fridge ready to bring out just before the party begins.

Arrange plates, bowls and glasses in your designated food area ready for your guests.

Put out any non-refrigerated items such as bowls of crisps and biscuits, but keep covered with cling film until the last minute.

Prepare your mocktails, punch etc. Keep refrigerated until the last minute.

Slice a few lemons and limes to add to drinks, and put them in bowls next to your glasses.

 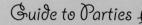

Personal party preparations

This is your big day, so make sure you leave plenty of time to make yourself look like a princess! You deserve it – the last thing you want is to be rushing around and getting all hot and bothered just before your guests arrive. You want to look fabulous, and looking fabulous takes time!

Princess

Make sure your boudoir is filled with all the things you will need to make yourself look stunning, put on some party music to get you in the mood and get pampering!

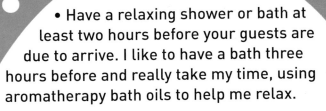

• Have a relaxing shower or bath at least two hours before your guests are due to arrive. I like to have a bath three hours before and really take my time, using aromatherapy bath oils to help me relax.

• Give yourself an all-over moisturise while your skin is still slightly damp, so that the moisture stays locked in. I love to use shimmery moisturiser which really catches the light and makes me look super sleek!

• Blow-dry your hair and style as you would like it. If you're going for volume, tip your head upside down to dry. If you want your hair to be sleek and straight, dry in sections and finish with hair straighteners.

• Give yourself a mani-pedi if you didn't manage to fit this in last night.

• Put your outfit on before applying your make-up to avoid smearing it on your clothes.

Party make-up

Party make-up is much more fun than everyday make-up. You can be as bold as you like, and there are lots of daring looks to try. If you want to try a completely new look, make sure you do a test-run a few days before to check you can manage it and that it suits you.

Foundation

You probably won't need much foundation. For best results make sure your face is cleansed and moisturised first, then apply foundation with your fingers. This will warm it up and make it easier to distribute evenly. Choose a foundation that is the same colour as your natural skin tone, not darker, as it will be too obvious.

Eyebrows

Pluck any stray hairs before you begin applying make-up to your eyebrows. Use an eyebrow pencil to define the shape of your brow and fill in any gaps, for a really sophisticated look. You can add eyebrow powder over the top of your pencil to help set it in place.

Eye shadow

Your eyes are the focal point of your face, so you want to get them looking perfect. When choosing what colour eye shadow to wear, always choose a different colour to your eye colour to make them stand out.

First, apply a light, neutral colour to your entire eye area from the upper lashes to the brow. This will help reduce creasing. Alternatively, you can use eye primer.

Use your darker colour on the lower lid, sweeping across from the inside corner of your eye to the edge.

Blend in so that the darker eye shadow follows the shape of your eye.

Eye liner

Eye liner can add a dramatic touch to your face, so it's perfect for parties. Use liquid liner for a precise line, or pencil liner to give your eyes a smoky finish.

On the upper lid, draw your line from the inner corner of your eye to the outer corner. If the line is too harsh, use a small brush to soften it. You can repeat if necessary.

On the lower lid, draw from the outside corner in.

Liquid eye liner can be difficult to apply as you need to be very precise, but practice makes perfect so have a go every day leading up to the party until you can draw a straight line. Keep cotton buds and eye make-up remover on hand to get rid of any smudges or mistakes.

Black and brown eye liners suit most people, but you can get all sorts of colours. White eye liner will give your eyes a wider, fresher look, whilst purple, blue or green will make them look electric!

Mascara

A flick of black or dark brown mascara gives your eyes the perfect finishing touch.

Remove the mascara wand from the tube and wipe any excess clumps off with a tissue.

Apply to your upper lashes from root to tip, in full strokes.

For a more dramatic look, apply two coats.

You need to be very careful when applying mascara to your lower lashes as they smudge more easily.

Remove the mascara wand from the tube and wipe as much mascara off with a tissue as possible.

If you are really worried about smudging, apply a thin film of Vaseline to the skin under your eyes first, using a cotton bud. This will protect your skin and help you wipe smudges away easily.

Apply to your lower lashes in a side to side motion, until all your lashes are covered.

If you're feeling really daring, go for a funky coloured mascara such as blue or green!

Lip gloss

After your eyes, your lips are the most important focal point of your face. Lip glosses really help to accentuate your lips, and are perfect for parties. You can go with a clear gloss, or pick a daring colour.

It's a good idea to apply lip balm to your lips before the gloss, so that they are smooth and moisturised.

Pout before applying lip gloss so you avoid getting it on your teeth – not a good look!

Starting in the middle of your mouth, apply the gloss in short strokes until both lips have been completely filled.

Blusher

Finish off your face with a touch of colour to your cheeks.
My golden blusher rule is never go too dark, as it won't suit you.
If you have pale or fair skin, use a light pink colour, but avoid bronzer.
If your skin is darker, you can use browner and redder tones.
Blusher is available in powder, cream and liquid forms. Liquid blush
is more difficult to remove if you make a mistake, whereas powders
and creams can be blotted off fairly easily.
Apply powder blusher with a brush, and cream and liquid blusher
with your fingers.
Start on the apple of the cheek and blend all the way back to your
hairline until you look naturally flushed.
Make sure you wash your hands after using
liquid blusher as it can stain!

Depending on your chosen outfit, you might like to add extra
details to your make-up.
Here are my top make-up tips for my favourite costumes:

Witch: green face paint, grey eye liner for warts
Vampire: lots of white face paint to make skin pale, black face
paint to create shadows under eyes, fake blood to trickle from the
corner of your mouth
Snow Queen: white face paint to make skin super pale,
false eye lashes, icy blue eye shadow and glittery pink lip gloss
Fairy: false eye lashes, lots and lots of glitter!
80s: bright coloured eye shadow over the whole lid
(two-tone works well), deep lipstick and lip liner,
fake mole over the top lip

Hostess with the mostest

You should be looking fabulous and ready to party in plenty of time for your guests to arrive. Start your party playlist going and make sure your party lights are on and any candles are lit. Now that everything's been taken care of, give yourself a final spritz of perfume and hairspray, and reward yourself and your friends with a mocktail!

Once your guests start to arrive, it's time for you to shine and be the perfect hostess!

Greet each guest personally, welcoming them into your home with a big smile.

Thank them when they tell you how fabulous you look (you really do!) and return the compliment.

Offer to take their coat, bags etc.

Show them into the main party area, and introduce them to anybody they don't know.

The key is to mingle. Greet each new guest but move on to the next person after a few minutes.

Once everybody has arrived, the fun and games can begin!

Remember to use your camera, and pass it round to your friends so they can take photos too.

Don't let any spillages or breakages ruin your night. It's a good idea to have cleaning products on standby just in case, but you can deal with any small messes after your guests have left.

If you want people to dance, be brave and lead the way onto the dance floor yourself.

Relax, smile and have fun! Your guests will follow your lead, so if you aren't having fun, nobody will!

Post-party
blues?

Post-party clean up

No excuses, it's got to be done! Start cleaning up as soon as you can after the party has finished. If you're too tired immediately after the party (I often am) you can always leave it till the morning after. If you've had friends sleeping over I'm sure they'll be happy to help you! Here's my post-party cleaning checklist:

- ♡ Open windows and doors to let in fresh air

- ♡ Go round every room with a bin bag and collect any rubbish

- ♡ Use a separate bag to collect anything recyclable

- ♡ Refrigerate any leftover food or drinks that haven't been sitting out too long

- ♡ Collect all non-disposable dishes and take to the kitchen to be washed

- ♡ Wipe down all surfaces

- ♡ Vacuum carpets, mop floors

- ♡ Address any stains that may have occurred (it's a good idea to have some carpet cleaner handy for those stubborn stains)

- ♡ Reward yourself with a relaxing bubble bath, then check out your presents and photos!

Present list

The day after your party can feel a bit depressing, but I always find making a present list really cheers me up!

Make a list of all the presents you received, and who they were from. This is guaranteed to make you smile, and will also come in handy when writing your thank you letters. Here's a present list I made last Christmas to give you an idea:

Guest: Edward
Present: CD
Comments: Must remember to lend him that new album I bought too, I know he'll love it!
Thank you note sent? Yes, 27th December

Guest: Anthony
Present: Year's subscription to fashion magazine
Comments: What a fabulous present!
Thank you note sent? Yes, 27th December

Guest: Helen
Present: DVD
Comments: I'm very impressed she remembered I wanted this.
Thank you note sent? No, need her new address!

Guest: Charlotte
Present: Perfume
Comments: Not my usual scent, but surprisingly I adore it!
Thank you note sent? Yes, 27th December

Thank you notes

I love creating my own thank you notes, and personalising each one. Here are some of my thank you notes from my birthday this year. I designed the paper myself!

Dear Chris,

I really love the bracelet you picked for me. It's beautiful, and goes perfectly with all my outfits so I can wear it every day.

Love, *Hello Kitty*
x

Dear Ben,

Thank you very much for the funky hat. It goes perfectly with my black waistcoat!

Love,

Hello Kitty
X

Even if someone has bought you a present that's not quite your thing, there's always a way to say thank you, and mean it!

Dear Alice,

The bird-spotting book you bought me is really educational, thank you. Every time I read it I will think of you.

Love,

Hello Kitty
X

Dear Milton,

Thank you very much for the bath salts. What an unusual scent!

Love,

Hello Kitty
X

Party photos

One of the best things about the end of a party is checking out all the fantastic photos!

Have your photos printed as soon as you can, or get them online on your FacePlace page! They will remind everyone what a fantastic time they had at your party and are great for a giggle! Check out some of mine below:

If you have any really nice pics of your friends, get duplicate copies printed for them, and include them with their thank you notes. They'll really appreciate the thought.

CUTIE PIE

Party diary

Make a party diary to record all your memories from the big night. Once you have printed your photos, you can stick these in too, so remember to leave plenty of space! You can also stick in one of your invitations and any leftover decorations. Here's my party diary from my spooky Halloween party:

4PM: Karen, Charlotte and Alice arrive to get ready and help me with all the last minute stuff. Mimmy joins us too, of course!

6PM: The party begins! Guests arrive on time.

6.30PM: Alice and Ben are having a dance-off already. Ben wins, because Alice trips up in her heels!

7.30PM: Phil's bat wings get tangled up in the fairy lights and we have to rescue him!

8PM: Mmm, food is delicious, even if I do say so myself. My cupcakes have disappeared already. Milton ate at least three!

8.30PM: Time for apple bobbing. Anthony wins.

8.45PM: Played the fastest game of Mummy Wrap ever. My team won, thanks to Edward who managed to stay really still.

9PM: Chris suggests we all play Truth or Dare, but he's sorry when he hears the question I have for him!

10.30PM: We've all been dancing for an hour! Dear Daniel is impressed by my moves.

MIDNIGHT: Time for everybody to leave. Except for Karen, Charlotte and Alice. They're sleeping over!

Spooky Halloween Bash
at Hello Kitty's Haunted Mansion

Date: 31st October
from six PM til midnight

Dress code: Come dressed as
your favourite dead celebrity!

RSVP: 0567 333 131
by 17th October.

1AM: Have pumped up airbeds and we're all snuggled up. Not quite ready to sleep yet, there's lots to talk about...

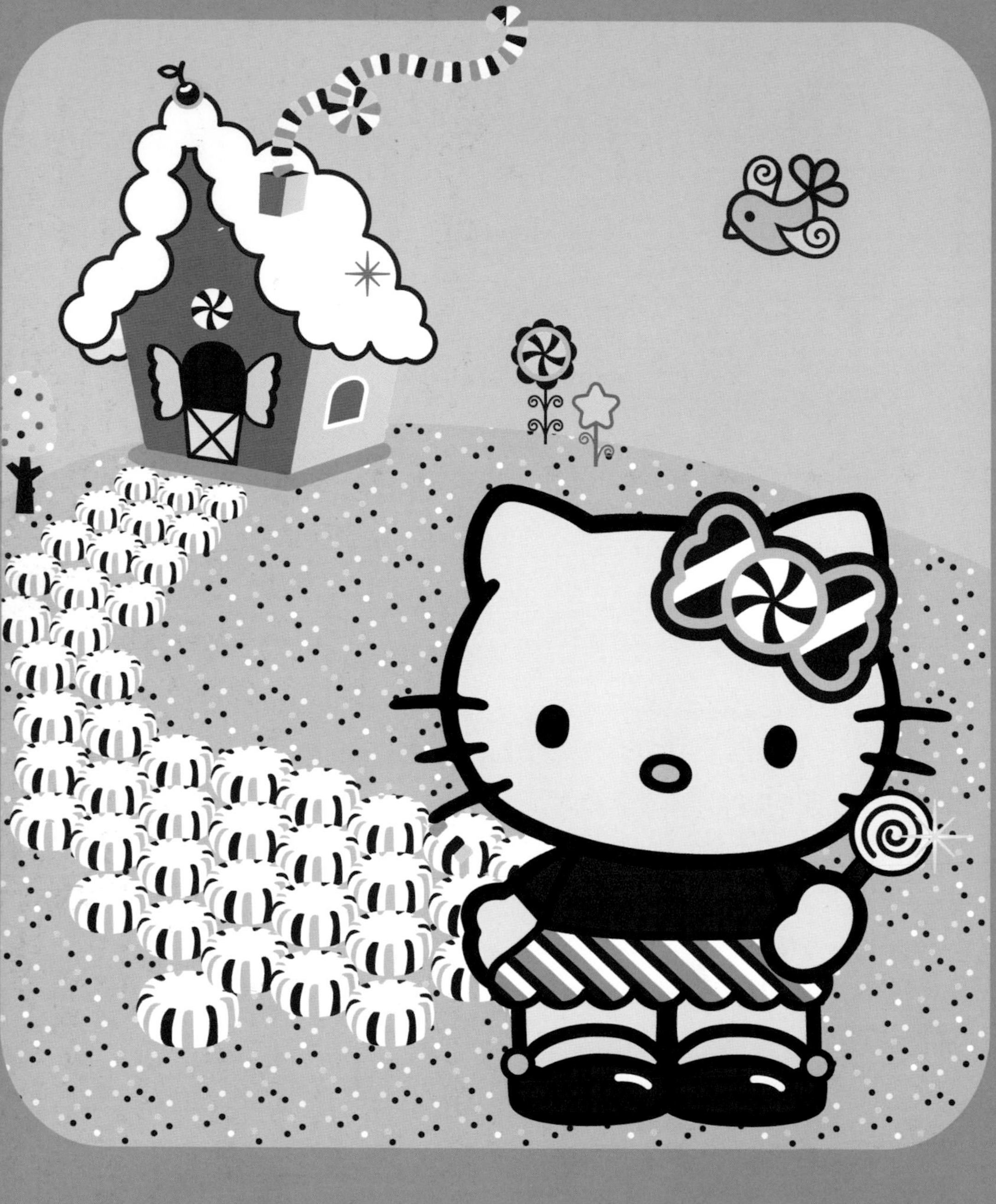

The perfect party guest

Looking fabulous

Being a guest at someone else's party means you have much more time to spend pampering yourself and getting ready. So invite one or two friends over to get ready with you, and enjoy!

Again, it's best to get your outfit sorted at least a week beforehand and make sure you have all the beauty and make-up supplies you need.

Here's my ultimate guide to get you looking fabulous on the day:

- Treat yourself to a lie-in so you'll be super-energised for later

- Have a filling and nutritious breakfast (scrambled eggs on brown toast and fruit is a favourite of mine, and a healthy energy booster)

- Put on some party music to get you in the mood

- Apply a cleansing or moisturising face mask, depending on your skin type

- Cover your hair in intensive conditioner and leave on for as long as possible

- Tie your conditioner-covered hair up while you have a bath using aromatherapy bath oils

- Give yourself an all-over body scrub

- Wash out intensive conditioner in the shower, then shampoo and condition as usual

- Apply body moisturiser as soon as you are out of the shower

- Have a healthy salad or soup for lunch (nothing too heavy if you will be eating lots of party food later)

- Wrap yourself in a robe and give yourself a pedicure (file your feet, trim and paint your nails)

- Give yourself a manicure next, allowing plenty of time for your nails to dry before doing anything else

- Hair can take a while to style if you're going with curls or an elaborate do, so it's best to make a start two hours before you have to leave

- Get dressed (leave your shoes off until you're ready to go to avoid aching feet)

- Apply your party make-up

- Put on your jewellery and any other accessories

- Give yourself a spritz of perfume

- Admire yourself in the mirror!

The party handbag

Every girl needs a handbag full of party essentials when venturing out to a friend's party. Party handbags are usually small and decorative (think stylish clutch rather than your usual over-the-shoulder tote) so you can only include the most essential items, such as:

- ♡ Mobile phone

- ♡ Money or bank cards

- ♡ House keys

- ♡ Make-up!

- ♡ Travel-size brush

Present ideas

I really love making home-made presents for my friends. Here are some of my favourite things to make:

Jewellery: I have a huge collection of strings, wires, beads and feathers, which I use to create all sorts of jewellery items. You can buy all these things from craft shops, and they are very cheap! Then you can design the perfect necklace or bracelet for your friend.

Bags: You can buy a plain bag and decorate it for a friend using glitter, adding beads and feathers to the zips, etc.

Photo magnets: Print out some silly photos of you and your friends. Buy some small round magnets, cut out your faces and stick them to the magnets. You've made a hilarious magnet set for your friend's fridge or notice board. What a great present to make them smile!

Recipes: If your friend is desperate for your white chocolate cookie recipe, why not type it up (or carefully hand write it) on some paper you've designed yourself and give it to them for their recipe file?

It's a wrap!

Now that you have the perfect present, you'll want to wrap it beautifully too. Wrapping can be tricky, particularly if your present is an odd shape. One way to get round this is to put your present in a box first, then wrap it. Alternatively you can use a pretty gift bag.

Here are some general guidelines to wrapping square or rectangular presents:

• Place the present face down on your wrapping paper (the paper should also be face down)

• Pull the paper over the present so that it covers the top side

• Roll the present onto its side, so that it is now completely covered by the paper

• Mark off how much paper you will need, then cut the paper. It's always best to cut slightly more than you think you will need

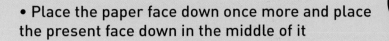

- Place the paper face down once more and place the present face down in the middle of it

- Take one edge of the paper and fold it over until it is in the middle of the upper side of the present, and is parallel with the side of the present

- Take the other edge and repeat. This edge should overlap the first slightly

- Hold the paper firmly in place and tape the overlap together

- Take one end of your present. Find the top edge of the present and press the paper down so it is flat against the side

- Fold the paper on either side of the end into the middle of the end, creating a triangle of paper at the bottom

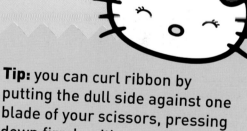

- Pull this up to cover the end of the present, and tape it firmly in place.

- Repeat for the other end

- Now you can add any other decorations, such as ribbon or gift tags to your present, and you're all done!

Tip: you can curl ribbon by putting the dull side against one blade of your scissors, pressing down firmly with your thumb, pulling the ribbon across the scissor blade while continuing to press with the thumb and then releasing the ribbon so that it springs into a pretty spiral.

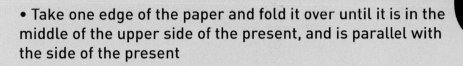

Make your own wrapping paper

Making your own wrapping paper can really give your gift that personal touch. You wouldn't want to turn up to the party with a beautifully wrapped present, only to find someone else had used the same paper, now would you? Plus, wrapping paper can be expensive, and there are so many fun ways to make your own which will cost you very little. (Younger Hello Kitty fans should always ask an adult to help them.)

Potato printing

I love this method!

You will need: paper, a few potatoes, a knife, a pen, and paint in various colours

• Decide on the shape you want to print on your paper. You can use as many as you like, in whatever pattern you like, so be creative
• Cut your potato in half so it has one flat side
• Draw your chosen shape onto the flat side of the potato
• Score round it with your knife and slice away at the surrounding potato until it is raised up from the rest of the potato
• Dip the potato into your paint, and print it onto your paper. Repeat to cover the whole sheet of paper
• Leave to dry for a few hours before wrapping your presents

Draw your own

There are no rules with this method. Simply draw whatever you fancy on a large sheet of paper, and get wrapping!

Decorative

You can add any manner of decorative details to sheets of plain paper. Last year I made some wrapping paper for Dear Daniel's Valentine's Day present. Here's how:

You will need: a large sheet of pink paper, a stack of old magazines, glitter, glue and confetti.

• Decide on a base pattern
• Add glue to the paper in this pattern
• Sprinkle glitter over your paper
• Brush any excess off. The glitter should stick to the glue in the pattern you chose
• Add more detail by sticking pictures from your magazines and confetti in between your glitter pattern, until you're happy with your design
• Leave to dry for a few hours before wrapping your present

These little unique touches will really make your present stand out, for all the right reasons!

Make your own cards

A card you have made yourself will mean much more to a friend than one you have bought, and will be just as beautiful. All you need is stiff paper, scissors, glue, coloured pens/pencils and decorations such as ribbon, glitter, swatches of material etc.

You can also make collage cards by cutting up old magazines, or use photos of you and your friends. There really are no rules to making cards, so take a look at some of mine below and get creative!

How to write birthday cards

When writing a birthday card, make it as personal to the recipient as you can. Nobody wants to receive a generic birthday message with no thought put into it. You may already know exactly what you want to say to your friend, but if not, here are some ideas to get you started:

Dear Fifi,

Happy Birthday! I'm really looking forward to your party. I have some great ideas for games we can play!

I hope all your birthday wishes come true this year. I can't wait to celebrate your special day with you. I'm sure I'll enjoy it as much as you will.

Love,

Hello Kitty

x

Dear Alice,

Happy Birthday! Let's celebrate how fabulous you are in style, with plenty of mocktails and dancing! I'm really looking forward to seeing your new kitten heels.

I hope you have a fabulous day, you deserve it.

Love,

Hello Kitty X

Dear Chris,

Have a fantastic day paintballing with the boys. We can't wait to party on down later and shower you with gifts! And we have a surprise for you…

Hello Kitty X

Love,

Party etiquette

Every party girl should know how to behave with class, so she'll always make the guest list. Manners go a long way! But just in case, here are the basics:

Never ignore an invitation!

Always RSVP within the stated time.

Always dress according to the instructions given on the invitation.

Bring a present and card for the host if it is a birthday, or, if it's any other celebration, a small token, such as your best home-made cookies or some pretty flowers, to show your thanks.

If it's a costume party, make the effort to dress up. Your host will really appreciate it!

It's OK to arrive slightly late to a party, but try not to arrive early. After all, you wouldn't appreciate it yourself.

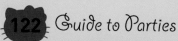

Once at the party, mingle! There will be lots of interesting people for you to talk to, so try to spend a little time with everyone.

Have fun!

Offer to help with the clean-up.

Don't be afraid to speak to people you don't know – everybody is there to have a good time and make new friends.

Thank the host before you leave, and make sure you tell them what a fantastic time you had.

Take a camera with you and try to take some photos throughout the night. Your host may be too busy to take very many and will really appreciate others helping to create fun memories of the big day.

Next time you have a party, make sure to return the invitation and invite the person who invited you.

Goodbye!

Well, it's time for me to start planning my next big bash. I hope you enjoyed my Guide to Parties. I had so much fun doing all the necessary research!

Whatever your next party will be, if you follow my tips I'm sure it will be a huge success! You never know, one day you might end up writing your own guide to parties based on all your experiences...

Lots of love,

Hello Kitty

x